SOUNDING THE ATLANTIC

OTHER POETRY BY MARTIN GALVIN

Wild Card (1989)

Making Beds (1989)

Appetites (2000)

Circling Out (2008)

SOUNDING THE ATLANTIC

MARTIN GALVIN

BRP
Broadkill River Press

COVER PHOTOGRAPH AND COVER DESIGN   Patric Pepper
AUTHOR PHOTOGRAPH   Theresa Galvin
TYPESETTING AND LAYOUT   Barbara Shaw

Library of Congress Control Number: 2010923239
ISBN 978-09826030-1-7

BRP
Broadkill River Press

James C.L. Brown,
Publisher
Broadkill River Press
104 Federal Street,
Milton, Delaware 19968
E-mail: the_broadkill_press@earthlink.net

TO THE IMMIGRANTS—
ALL OF US

ACKNOWLEDGMENTS

Grateful acknowledgments are due to the editors of the following journals in which these poems first appeared, some in different form:

Alembic, "Screened Bird"

Argestes, "After the Battle at Seven Pines," "Office Visit," "Saying Goodbye," "The Big Leagues"

Atlantic Monthly, "Passive Aggressive"

BigCityLit, "Enough"

Bogg, "Coblentz's Farm"

Broadkill Review, "The Season After and Just Before," "Playthings," "Blind Girl," "Harley Rider at Rehoboth Beach," "The Egg Man in Warsaw," "First Car in a Young Country"

Common Ground, "Aioi Bridge, Hiroshima, 1984"

Commonweal, "Still Life Study," "Heron Bay," "Leaf Raker," "Army Sawbones"

Country Mouse, "Baloney Sandwiches"

Delmarva Quarterly, "Artisan," "Beyond the Hot Sun," "Corn Stalk," "Weekday Morning," "Catching the Waves," "Soundings Near the Atlantic"

Feila-Festa, "Antietam's Bloody Lane"

FRiGG, "Goat Farming at Flat Rock," "Summer Spikes"

G.W. Review, "The Burghers of Calais"

The Innisfree Poetry Journal, "Candidate," "Maude Remembering," "Spider Webs," "Trapeze Artist Under the Big Top," "Epiphany on a Gentle Day," "Cranes in Flight Over Warsaw," "Practicing the Art in New Jersey," "Fatback"

Isotope, "The Scientist's Prayer"

King's English, "Gravities"

National Honors Report, "Blueberry Woman"

New Republic, "Apprentice Chef," "The Purposes of Circuses"

New Verse News, "Advice to War Poets"

Ohio Journal, "Clam Shucker"

Painted Bride Quarterly, "The Silence of Eggs"

Perigee-Arts Magazine, "Finding Loss in a Flemish School"

Petroglyph, "*The Man with the Hoe* at the Getty Museum"

Poet & Critic, "Enough"

Poet Lore, "Mary Cassatt," "Hilda & Me & Hazel"

Poetry, "Marathoner," "Widower at Work"

Potomac Review, "At Their Math," "Geography Lesson"

Red Rock Review, "Viewpoints"

Science '84, "Doorman"

Sow's Ear Poetry Review, "Cream"

Vulgata, "Weathering the Front Door"

Zone 3, "Ox-Eye Daisies"

GRATITUDES

Warm and special thanks to the many smart and generous people who have helped me with my poems:

To Sid Gold and Jamie Brown for their courage and faith in these poems

To Theresa, my first reader and clearest seer

To Rod Jellema for the high polish he brings to dull metals

To Mary Ann Larkin and Patric Pepper for their fine taste, expertise and generosity

To Kay Voss, my NYC listening post who gets it all

To Barbara Shaw for her patience, kindness and precision in typesetting

To each of my students and teachers

To Yaddo for the dedicated time and creative space to complete this manuscript

INTRODUCTION

MARTIN GALVIN reminds us that poems say things the way most people would say them if only they could.

In conversation with the reader, many of these poems have a voice that rings with a slight Irish lilt, echoing his boyhood neighborhood in Philadelphia. But rising out of that, the voice is almost always quirky and folksy, angular and hooked, and yet somehow surprising and tender and lyrical.

> *Got nose to nose with ants, I did,*
> *to get our signals straight about our needs.*

It is often his ear for such syntax and cadences in the plainness of speech that gives his lines the economy all talkers must envy. Hear how he catches an old man near the sea who

> *lets himself be seen for what he is,*
> *and shrugs for what he isn't anymore.*

Galvin's voices sound out with sharp edges what they observe with compassion and insight: a clown resigning from the circus, a monk who gathers eggs, a place in winter silence ("Heron Bay"), a few paintings, the glory of cows ("Cream"), a "Clam Shucker." While there is much joy in the world he is sounding, he is astonishingly evocative of the inhumanity in past wars he never saw (pages 34 – 39), experiencing them more fully and intently than most on-scene reporters could ever have recorded them. I had to wonder for wonderful moments while reading this book just how in hell he got the feel of Warsaw in 1943 (at age six?) and how he could have been so fully a human presence in the American Civil War at Seven Pines in 1864. The simple truth is, he knows how to ride the currents of words to take him inside anything. The very sounds of words and his passion for mining and arranging them sharpen his social sensitivity and deepen his sense of history—and in the same way evolve in his work the very personal moments of wistfulness and whimsy.

Although his 1989 book *Wild Card* was selected as a prize-winner by the greatly respected poet and critic Howard Nemerov, and although he has published four fine chapbooks of poetry and more than four hundred poems in literary magazines including *The Atlantic Monthly, Commonweal, Poetry,* and *The New Republic,* Galvin has received far too little recognition. His workload as a dedicated teacher did not leave much time for making and promoting the big books that might have displaced the chapbooks. Finally, in this book of soundings (both meanings please), we get a full and important collection of his work.

And yes, I do mean important. As he paces the wide range of this book, simply mining the workings of words, he gives us the leaps and pleasures of mind unique to the reading of poems. But Galvin is also the kind of poet who cuts his way into—and takes us into—where we have almost but never quite been before. The poems—the voices—are making discoveries about our world and ourselves to which we have no other access. And that to me is the true value of poetry, and why poets write it.

– Rod Jellema

CONTENTS

SOUNDING THE ATLANTIC

CLOWN FACE

Easter Monday, calendar wise, the clown
who plies his trade in the circus parade,
Whose face grew up from crowded shoulders
In a public place, declares he has had enough
Of scaring little children, will put away
Forever the paints that name him clown.

The crooked old woman who depends so
On him could not have been less pleased,
Nor is the Master clown, who has made
For him allowances, granted benefits
And named him driver of the clown mobile.
They love him for themselves, for his face
In which they see a terror they can share.

Listen yourself and you will hear
the old woman worry the rocking chair.
You too may wonder at the clown's turn
away from the danger of laughter,
and how a man who does so well what he does
can hope to find another way to have a living
and so deny to children the tightrope of fear
they need a little more than they want joy.

PASSIVE AGGRESSIVE

A 15 yr old girl speaks

It's like I just like have to kiss
a boy in every city where I am like at.
It's just so totally like I do this. Kiss.
So I am like last year? in Florence?
Italy? So weird.

I mean totally it was like so weird
I hadn't like kissed like one of them?
And I was so totally like bummed.

So I see this really like old man
at the airport and like it's what
I do so I go totally up to him and like
kiss him and it was totally like weird.

He was like twenty-seven and his wife—
it was like Like. She was so
passive aggressive. Like sulked.

I was just like. It was like I did it?
Like totally kept my kiss list going? Weird.

LEAF RAKER

She gathers up what nature's left for us
because our houses touch on hers.

Thin as a broom, she sweeps whatever falls
almost as well as the wind, intent on giving shape

to what is left of autumn. Every year
it works. When winter wakes us to surprise

and weathers in our street, she shovels off
the snow covering up those tracks that lead

to us. We call her the quixotress of trees,
mistress of drifts, as if we could shrug off

the way she puts the neighborhood to rights.
Without our leave, she works against the clock

to shape a street that otherwise would fail
to find itself beneath the swarm of falls.

Spring and summer both, she sprinkles seed to meet
the rain. She plugs the ground around our trees

with fertilizers, waits for the magic to happen
to maple, oak and elm, then she gathers up

her autumn tools and sets to work. While she rakes,
she praises the sky for seasons, us for being here.

MARATHONER

He hammered his heart until it was ready,
smeared some ointment where it was meant
to be and where it wasn't, laved it on his breath,

his child's favorite soap pipe, his eyes, his teeth,
the belly he'd sooner not have, the spooned meat
for the dog that had to come with him.

He flexed the bald soles of his bottommost bones,
his toes curling in as though afraid
of what was coming, then accepting the burden.

He did the required elongations, the rotations
his training manual forgot, readied his suspensions
of disbelief at what he was about to do,

steeled his eye and the muscles he could reach,
said his kneeldown prayers and faretheewells
and set off, as if a gun had told him, Go.

HARLEY RIDER AT REHOBOTH BEACH

I try to read the scars he wears as map
enough to tell me where he has been.

What's broken into me doesn't like
the tattoos that he has stitched into his chest,

just above the nipples. *Born to Die*, one boasts,
the other *Hell Hound*. That night, she whispers

sweetly nothings in my ear of how it feels
to sleep with a hell hound born to die.

Next day, I stand beside him in the surf,
trading stories of other Mains, a storm

that lasted days and finally tossed us up,
the way a Harley can hurt a man.

I might as well tell you now
While I can still be heard above
The slap and thwack of the racquet, the *pick-
Ed-de-pock* of the ball as exclamation mark,
The squeal and squeak and fffst of turn
And stop. What's needed here is skill
And speed and—you might as well accept it—
Luck, luck in the gut, in the ankle and wrist,
And a sharp shiver of the eye
That you either have or have not got.

Bring razors of wit to this tight room
Then, and an opponent worth that part
Of a life's luck you'll have to give up
So the art can be allowed its turn.
The angles matter as they always do.
Study yourself to get these down, be
As oblique, as acute, as you know how.
You'll need too a tolerance for sound
And the various colors of silence.

A sense of diplomatic grace will help
As you address the ball, the wall,
Your manner of approaching the line
That has been drawn by other men.
Just one thing more before we start:
This game is brief. Soon enough,
If you listen up, you'll know the score.

OFFICE VISIT

There's one thing many doctors hate enough to say.
Ask yours about his own preoccupying pain.

If you promise to pay, he will tell you that it's pure
and as fragile as a spinster aunt, grown poor

and speckled gray with ancient losses.
My psychiatrist protests that there is less

to his problem than he wanted. He would rather
every habit would be worse than his father's.

How the smell of his nurse curls into his hair
makes my bone man shave his arms and wish her

Ivory clean. He tells me his wife has a passion
for manifest pistils and manifold stamens

and makes him poison that that would kill her blooms.
When she hears her knife-hand knuckles creak,

my surgeon thinks of vises and the cracking
voice she has and means to lose. The radiologist

has a smile tucked inside her dimple, detests
the multiplying malignant cells of men.

My neurologist tells me only what is certain:
The two of us will go to many doctors in our time.

He hopes I have the craft to mute my rage
and the art to suffer all of theirs with grace.

STILL LIFE STUDY

An apprentice to the craft could draw
you, perfect squirrel, in motion,
your belly slung low in a physics right
for one of your size and disposition.
It's plain the tree was your retreat
in the hawk-lit woods, your helmeted head
poised to see threats coming,
peripherals keened by art beyond ours.

How right to be a squirrel in such a place,
your face as full of pleasure as the nut
filling the shell. What prodigious leaps,
what sheers of will, flinging yourself
from done branch to undone. Still, in the tree-
less world you run a fatal risk. Tires
blind and straight as crutches don't go for craft,
your fake left, go left. They round their lives
in a minor league, leave you a question mark.
No skill to that sport, nothing worth your move.

CREAM

She likes to remember the cows
for the steam that rises from them
autumn and spring as if their mouths
were all of them, as if their bodies
were locomotives, starting up again,
as if they were the earth itself,
rising into clouds, becoming rain,
machines, as clean and right as when
machines were new and quiet in the world,
knew when to move and when to rest,
spent much of their being waiting to be,
the dumb power a gentle hum on the earth,
making a name by simply being there.

She likes to think of them as sisters
to her, lying down, half-drowsed
in pasture, ready to be something else,
and rising together to walk with her
into the houses of men, another life.

She sees them now, their large heads
placid and heavy on their settled bodies,
grouped under a tree as if for a painting,
their browns and whites blending into the soft
shades of spring the painter has made for them,
and moves herself as in a dream of cow,
across the fence, across the meadow.
She means to lie down in their midst,
the hot flanks breathing on her skin,
and go to sleep. When she wakes, her face
will be licked clean and in her hands
the warm teats will swell and gush.
She will wash like the queen of hearts in cream.

HERON BAY

There is a space for winter here
To grow its ice. There is a place
For a small boat with oars and sail.
There is a piece of water here
For a fish farmer and his old wife,
Turned by the wind into the wind.
We say the night heron stands and waits
For breaking water. He knows that water yields,
That fishes break. His neck is a white slake
Fishing for the water's sake and his.
He takes only his place which is as small
As he needs. He leaves the rest to you
And me, a small boat, winter and a pair
Of old crabbers leaning into the wind,
Space for oceans to turn in, things that bend.

VIEWPOINTS

Someday I will walk these woods
With an old woman, as quiet
And crooked as twigs in the wind,
The two of us, and like the wind
Stop when we have to and turn
To the house for a moment
Before we continue doing
What we want to: wave and applaud
And kiss or piss as our needs announce.

A Passer-by will shake his refurbished head
In disbelief, happy anyway for a daytime story
He can tell his dinner friends.
No one will believe the thing he saw today,
Though what he saw is true as afternoon:
Two dodderers, dallying along a path,
Cheering what anyone with sense would fear.
They were two of a kind he'd never seen before,
Kissing and pissing like they were natural things.

PLAYTHINGS

The Midwestern woman loved deep snow
and holy days but hated with some heat the men
she built when she was in her twenties,

their stony, glazed stares at her house,
the way they fell apart in chunks
when she threw her arms around them.

Her father built them shelter out of stone and dirt
that never fell down even when the ground
shook beneath the house when he dropped dead.

Her friend though, the one from Sanibel,
loved the idea of snowmen more than the Gulf
of Mexico, the way it slavered at her feet.

She has shaped and spaced a hill of sandmen
but never thought to show a single one how
to cool her down when she surrounded him.

Before she reached puberty, a hurricane
in its waning tore her t-shirt off and made
her love the sting of sand on her frightened chest.

Ever since, she has held in some contempt
the placid days of spring when calm warmth
woos the flowers into fleeting pretty being.

Sand and snow, the crystals fall at the woman's feet
spent as swept palms. A sorry sight, those sorry men,
enough to make a woman yearn for other weathers.

OX-EYE DAISIES

Early morning, I met my grandmother in my Friday dream
Of being ten again. She has been dead for fifty years,
Which neither of us thought mattered much,
The way loss will. She had just found her glasses
Where she had left them, on her nose.

At the matinee, it's early autumn there and here
The white wood aster and the white-topped sedge
Have given up their showy parts and gone to seed.
I tell her I forget her maiden name and that I miss
More than my eye teeth the comfort of her lap.

She says I should not expect much from her
But a bit of memory and that her name from before I was
Was Mary Margaret Macgillicuddy,
Though she's not sure she'd ever told her husband,
He not being a musical man.

The actresses are skinny things, locked in a hug and a kiss,
Not that we care about the mush. The usher tells us
Shush. That we will have to shush or leave.
Shush, Macgillicuddy says, is a word your mother loved.
The way it tickled the air above her tongue made her laugh.

We do. We quiet down like horses after a hard run
Until the next love scene and then we are up and out of there.
The usher who said shush gives her a bouquet of ox-eye
Daisies and spider lilies to beg forgiveness for the job
He has to do, says she minds him of a girl he almost married.

Outside, the flowers remember before us what season it is.
I find the note the usher wrote to her about the farm
He loved to work before he had to leave. While I watch
It curls up like brown years, like the delicate words
My mother left on the doorstep, like broken leaves.

CLAM SHUCKER

Her gnarled knuckles figure out her age.
She has worked many things, has sewn the breasts
of turkeys back together each November
of almost sixty years, has broken necks
of chickens when she's had to, and for the life
of her, she's shucked an ocean full of clams.

The cold of a hundred fathoms works into her bones
like sly eels. Sometimes the rust of sunken ships
comes drifting to the tips of her fingers, then
she flexes them like puppets, making songs
to match the waking shapes. Sailors, brown
and full of spice, walk the line toward her.

At times her hand sits, a foreign country
that has occupied her, a brazen toad squat
and lewd in her green lap. But then the shapes
come slipping in between the swollen cracks
like treasure undersea, like dead men
rising with the tide. Those songs are hers

that give the frozen knuckles hope to add,
such songs that swelling burst and break
her fingers loose, that send the writhing eels
wrinkling back to sea, that mend the shells
and broken wings flapping in her fluid bones.

SOUNDINGS NEAR THE ATLANTIC

The man of many trousers is no fool, pulls over
for the Rescue Squad's red blare that means what it says.
He is still and stopped in the kind of groove
he hoped he had left in the city, at work, away
from this corn and chicken town two miles west
of the easy rock and roll of the breaking Atlantic.

A carload of outraged music and teenage boys
trails in the wake of the ambulance, their radio
speaking decibels for them about the mess it is
being a teenage boy, the sounds they know
are coming before they give themselves away.

He has been granted the ear to think that the crickets
in his pear tree make as much noise as horny boys,
and for the same basic reasons. The last time
he was surprised by sound, a girl with hair as long
as winter breath had come up behind and passed

him on the boardwalk, her bare feet whispering
threats different and more serious than the slap
and pause slap and pause of his loose sandals.
A man of sungrown freckles takes the morning kite
to air to get a feel for what the weather promises

for his shored kids, reeling the string with slow regard
for the gulls, that he not strangle one by accident
and add too early to the shore's run of scalloped edges.
He has heard his daughter lecture even God about the care
of living things and he, decidedly this morning, is not He.

The locals have a word or two for us, the walkers on their sand,
the crowded talkers on the boardwalk they alone have wintered,

they and the skittering gulls and the lapping sea. The chicken
    skinners
teach their kids the language that they use to get the city folk
    into focus.
The kids have a language of their own—for us and for their
    parents both.

The oldest men mumble in their sleep soft prayers they
    learned
when silence circled the country fields like chicken hawks.
When she is called to speak at the PTA, a daughter of the town
complains about the new teacher who has come from
    Baltimore
and never been to church one time. The babies don't have the
    words

yet but their tongues itch to get at the bitter home-made cider.
Near the bearding corn, the wings of a hummingbird wind up
the air to such a pitch that a dragonfly squadron starts their
    engines.
The Atlantic feathers the beach with whispers from the East.
Something older than gossip is about to be heard.

WEEKDAY MORNING

For Steve Knox
b. 10/10/1910 – d.10/10/2006

Stooped as a willow branch
from gravity, he measures his walk
and the pulls of cultivation,
the kinds of pleasure a country man
can bear, leaning down to nurture
flowers of broccoli, rows of waxbeans,
the convoluted vines that hide tomatoes
from the birds and too much sun,
mounding the homes of russet potatoes.

He can't see so well. The one eye
tricks him when he isn't looking, turns
things double. He takes his time
a weekday morning picking cucumbers
and carrots, numbering his find,
   a gather for his oldest daughter in Baltimore,
   and one for the baby who never quite grew up,
   the biggest for his wife of sixty-six years.

When he is ready, the new pick bunched
in one hand, the latest fruit of narrowing rows,
he brings them like flowers to the kitchen door.
She takes them thinking of the canning ahead,
that she is getting slow for a girl's work,
tells him to wash his hands and sit to table,
the eggs are getting cold, he needs his grits.

WIDOWER AT WORK

He has promised her he will practice for years
the ways to get along with fewer breaths,
will fill his lungs and find himself a flat place
for when the room begins to move around him,
the floor tilt as if it means to open up. He gives
strings of spaghetti the same spare treatment
now. He draws them up one at a time
from the dinner plate's straggle,
each moment of concentration brought
to the tight seine of his teeth keeps
him thin, he tells himself, this taking time.

When he was twenty his father told him
no good would come of holding on.
His teacher, a painter of absences and loss,
pretended no less. Evenings, he watches the war
of the cars, the street light move shadows
across the wall and he hums a child's song
to the saint whose name he carries to keep her safe.

He will argue with that melody some time
tomorrow but that will be soon enough,
after he has done his bow-downs in the sun.
Such contradictions are the only things
he has come to love, the sweat opening
to welcome its brother the rain. He helps
the voice of her memory walk across the road
after dinner as the night owls come awake
to what is left of the backyard's day.

BLUEBERRY WOMAN

The blueberry woman has wrecked her week
and the kitchen, baking muffins, baking pies.
She reeks of blueberry jam, has steeped herself
with thoughts of blood and bloody butcherings.
What she comes to at the end, and prints
in blue juice on the bathroom door,
is the family's menu for the harvest month.

Her children, home for lunch and stuffed
with chalk, a permanent peanutbutter glaze
to their eyes, are served up to their regret
grilled blueberries *au gratin*, blueberry soup,
blueberry tart in blueberry juice, then spooned
out the door and back to school, their faces
drained, their mouths as dyed as grief.

Her husband attachés his way from work, dulled
to boldness by drinks with the boys. What he
expects for dinner is baked potatoes,
New York Strip, asparagus with hollandaise.
He also expects the kids to be fed and bathed
and ready for bed and his wife dressed up
for dessert and ready, by god, to roll. She is.

She darkens up what is dull about the meal.
What he gets is blueberries *a la carte*.
Blueberry hash he gets and blueberry toast
and blueberry sauce for the blueberry mousse.
As he nods off in bed she leaves him lack
and blue. Dressed to kill, she heads outside.
A blue moon ripens in the letting sky.

In that new light, she murders what
she can; the strawberry beds,
the blueberry patch, rows and rows
of tomatoes. Come the next harvest,
her family can eat flowers, as far as she's
concerned. Roots they can eat, or seeds,
rainbows, daffodils, stripes of the blue moon.

TRAPEZE ARTIST UNDER THE BIG TOP

Fellina the Falling Star
performs her life-defying swoops
and swings above the center ring.

Gainers, Double Gainers, Jack-
Knives, Flips, she does them all,
finds momentum in the letting go,

remembers one time one platform
next time the other, the view toward
a farther side beyond what we can see.

And in between, the slippery bar awaits her,
like yours and mine who every time
hold on to nothing more than air.

She recovers on the backward swing
and sometimes on the downward rush
exults with a joy that we can fathom.

Nothing is guaranteed under the Big Top,
only the momentary stop,
the catching on beyond the letting go.

BLIND GIRL

If you've not run your face into a wall,
I've never spit a gun at birds
           or hit a deer

before its chance to move into the mottle
and I can tell the truth of deeper blue
better than you can ever shout
              of red that awful red.

While I've not seen your shapes and sizes,
you have not plumbed the depths of black
I have behind my eyes, the ways
they talk and walk me through the steps
              I need and want to dance.

Describe for me the color of clean.
I'll tell you how a scrubbing feels inside.
And when you see the conductor raise his stick,
I'll tell you how the hidden drums will march
             to wake the sleepy violins.

FIRST CAR IN A YOUNG COUNTRY

The young man, jutjawed and certain,
tells his new wife, she of the long hair
and longer dreams, that he must buy a car,
that they must go to his mother's funeral,
and she should dress the older chicken
for them to bring to celebrate the life.

She, being a bride, takes the axe
to the chicken's neck as she must,
plucks the feathers and scrubs the skin,
puts on her long brown dress and a borrowed veil.
Bread and their chapped bible go with the chicken
into a swaddle. On the porch in a straight chair

she waits for his return, and in good time he does,
driving a polished dented hearse,
as black as a coal mine at night, shining
freckled around the seams with rust.
His mother will be glad they have come,
his sisters say, and what a fine fiddle
of a car to ride them all to the grave.

Two days after the laying down, his grief
insufficient for a husband with plans,
he takes the hearse back to the used car lot,
says it won't do at all. He needs a happy coupe
he means to fill with a brood of little ones
to take the place of the chicken and the past,
a winged sedan, a racing stripe and money back.

AT THEIR MATH

Geometry class filled up with secrets.
As domestic as cats, as clever as cobwebs,
they assumed the odd corners of the room.

They walked the rows of desks listening for reasons,
little brothers with nothing to do but do
what they were doing; as pleased with themselves

as old men who have found something important
to do with their afternoon. They found their way
like cheap perfume into the heavy air, dropping hints

of themselves on the heads of the teacher and her aide.
The secrets smelled of ammonia and elixir of chocolate,
as if they'd come from chemistry and home ec.

Wherever they went they threaded through
soft nasal passages into brains that would have been
happier settling in on the cusp between A and B,

on the thin edge where, if they fell, they'd only be
someplace within the heart of a triangle with a problem
simple enough for a clever equation and no talk necessary.

BALONEY SANDWICHES

The night fiend with the pale blue complexion
Lived under my bed when I was nine
And old enough to dress for church and multiply
By eights. He reminded me of sour milk
So while I did not fear him, I feared his smell
And how I used to gag on Monday mornings
When I drank cod liver oil. My sister watched,
Her pigtails like a metronome of No.

I'd talk to him despite the smell sometimes,
Recounting my grievances against cruel fate
And an old aunt who smelled like mustard.
Once I invited him to show himself and fight.
He said *I'm the night fiend, Dope,* and went to sleep.
Did I say he sharpened his nails on the springs
And sang to himself the old ghoul songs?

I was a terrible lot of a lad.
My best friend popped me in the nose
Because he talked like brakes
were in his throat and I laughed.
Roses grow best in chicken poop
My mother said. Imagine that. Poop.
The night fiend went into the army when
I turned ten. Good thing, too.
This growing up took all my wits.

TEACHER'S PET

My Johnny ain't no rose. Learn him. Don't smell him.
—Parent to teacher at PTA 1898

These mountain women. Come in here, I swear,
Like wild goats and tell us how to teach their kids.

The men are just as bad, grunting and belching
Straight through my preparation. The pigs.

I'd like to see that mother try to show a strapping boy
How to find the hypotenuse of a triangle,

Lean down to him and guide his hand
When he stinks like a stuck toilet, nothing less.

I'd just like to see her. And the father too
Though what I heard, he has gone to the city

These two months past, taking his own smell
With him and good riddance. Maybe I can do

What's right by holding Roddy back. Teach him how
To speak himself right clear and practice pen-

Manship. It's more than that mother will do,
For sure. And besides, he's big enough

To shoe a horse. It's about time he learned
There's other ways a woman can be

Than her ill-favored ways. I swear to cheese
Her Roddy is a boy worth keeping on

Through harvest time. At least by then he's grown
And ready for those wagons coming down the road.

EPIPHANY ON A GENTLE DAY

I had just finished writing an introduction to a Fred Astaire con-
cert, when out of the solid block of wood emerged a cat—supple,
lithe, friendly, gray, Egyptian in his regality—the artist walked over
and slit an eye in the eyeless head and gave this feline perfection
life. He stalked and curled, posed and postured as cats do, then,
someone decided he should return to the block of wood—he
curled back into the part left vacant by his recent emergence, took
a while to position himself with head on front paws, then merged
back into the wood like a disappearing fog on a landscape.

You know as well as I the ways dreams happen,
Your student had just finished writing an introduction
To a Fred Astaire concert, when out of the solid block of wood
Emerged a cat—supple, lithe, friendly, gray,
Egyptian in his regality, whistling Dixie.

The sculptor walked over and slit an eye in the anvilled head
And gave, as if he gave nothing, perfection to his work.
He stalked and curled, posed and postured as cats do,
Then deciding he should return to the block of wood.
He curled back into the part left vacant by the artist,

Took a while to position himself, the way cats will,
Head on front paws, haunches raised at rest,
Eyes purring about himself, how right he is,
Then merged back into the wood
        Like a disappearing fog on a morning shore.

        Once, an Irishman in Kinvarra walked toward me
        In soft rain. "A gentle day," he nodded, and went on.
        That stolid man, as solid as a farm, real as a clenched pipe,
        I've heard mutter his benediction to my stranger self
        These many years, the two of us for a moment found.

SCREENED BIRD

A curious bird invaded our vacant space
This early spring, made the usual mockery
Of the screen door's need to keep
The outside out, slipped through and killed
Herself for the vision that she had.

No harm in that except the summer porch
Meant for sitting in and looking out
Became her slaughter house. Another bird
I almost met a couple of years ago
Died in our attic, battered by studs,

Pierced by roofing nails, surrounded
by the hard and dark with nothing to drink
But mouse droppings, nothing to eat
But silverfish. Expected death. Okey-dokey,
A way to go where he had to anyway. But to live

Like this other one for weeks inside a place
Where light is all around, the walls soft lies,
Is close enough to our brief passings-by you'd think
I'd sympathize, find common ground
With Icarus and this dark starling. I don't.

I use the iron shovel for her bier, to dig the hole,
For the distance that I have been told to keep
Her germs away from mine, from such a cleaning
Up that might mean death inside and out. I sweep
The feathers into a pile for the kids to understand
The corner where we found her, I teach right angles,

Newton's Laws. The crescent left in the screen as record
Of her passing through and how and where has been
Repaired. We're safe enough from bugs to sit out now.
All summer long, I read the dropping sky for songs
But nothing comes except some show-off storms.
Now and then in sleep or half awake, I hear her flap
Of fury against the attic floor and know that dreams
Are stirring up the joys of being blind, with wings.

Since, being left handed, he couldn't play
Second base, he caught a leaf, a single Vee-
Veined leaf, and then, from a bird
Who had flied out

He caught a white feather, and once,
A fish that flopped in his hand
And lay still as a spent penny,
One eye at a time accusing him,
Him who played left field, flat-eyed
As a window at what was coming.

He caught an acorn from a prudent squirrel
And tucked it in his pocket to keep the cold
Coins company, caught a bit of a hint
the season was over.

He caught a faint drumbeat, a sign
The rain is kind enough to let him hear
When there is nothing left on the dugout roof
But itself and the late September night,
Those soft reminders,
Those polished catchers.

MAUDE REMEMBERING

The girl with a memory as long
as her finger dials L.A. by mistake.
The man on the other end of the line,
a man with murder on his mind,
blood on his tongue, wants to make

a date. His voice sharpens in her ear
as if he means to pick her clean,
reminds her of something she does not want
to want to do. As absentminded as tomorrow,
she agrees to meet him, makes promises,

gives him the name she's always wished
she had been named instead of Maude,
and an address someplace in Encino.
She's never been there but she loves the hiss
of it. She hangs up quickly, soon

is sad she didn't get his name and number,
being almost as ready as she has ever been
to recall what's past, even the warning tone
of her mother's voice telling her things
she is sure to forget as long as she lives.

CORN STALK

We talk things over as if I know what's what,
making our judgments about the Silver Queen,
about the weathers we just have had or will,
as if we share an interest that will multiply
with friendly talk about nothing much that we can change.

"The wind'll lay the corn down," my neighbor says,
and shakes his head at such a truth, at fatal chance,
at his crop in just that place, at just that height. The wind.
"Best stand I ever had," he says, and he a grower now
for fifty years. I spend most of my time confusing fact

with metaphor and forgetting what I should not, but
I know a good thing when I've heard it, can hardly wait
to get away to write what is passing through, afraid that I
will miss my chance. While I'm inside the wind decides
not now and turns around. The corn waves goodbye,

the farmer and his wife take mine to lunch, leave me
talking to myself, hunched over like a cow at feed.

PARTING THE AIR

You swallow chewing gum, the mother says,
Your blood and bones will bunch together
The kidneys lock in what it should let out,
The stomach stick to the pancreas. You'll clog

Your joints so tight you can't make a move
Especially on the court when you want to fake
Left go left, have to stand where you are
Till you aren't. What the father says:

You swallow a watermelon seed, that's it,
Like an unmilked udder, like your brother's balloon,
Bigger and bigger until you're about to burst
And you will. You're a cat, you swallow grass,

You've seen what happened to our calico. Like that.
You swallow someone's line, you're a flopped fish,
You're a bird with a toothache instead of a fish,
you're hooked, done for. You'd be better off to bite

Your own tongue before you do that, eat your good shirt,
Swallow your words before you do that.
Let me ask you this: you ever see a swallow fly
Above a field of young chewing gum?

He keeps going, right? Would not stop for a Wrigley's
Even if you gave it to him free for nothing. Smart,
That bird, eating his flies on the fly,
Making his way from here to there, parting the air.

SUMMER SPIKES

When I was twelve, I spiked a boy at second base,
Put that season's cleats against an ear
And turned the key until it caught. That coach.

He knew the game, got us in the playoffs,
Three years straight. I'm not blaming him,
Not giving him the credit, either.

The score was tied, as it often was
That year in Philly, zip to zip,
Apples marked the left field line.

A few of us had smarted from the tongue
Of Mary Mary, a girl whose name
Was all she had, that and the nerve

To put her mouth against a boy's
And talk the kind of talk
Would never pass for infield chatter.

So I spiked him, put my cleats down hard,
Slid like someone I'd never met, nor want to.
The wind blew in from left, the surest sign

Autumn was coming and the end of games.
After it was over, I sat on the stained ground
And ate sickle pears, stunted, half-grown.

CATCHING THE WAVES

We watch boys of the right age and place
Straddle their surfboards, marking time, sizing up
swells until the right wave makes toward them
like an ancient god with curled lip and strength
beyond their knowing. They turn, then,
and paddle like hell's behind them, heaven or hell,
and they've a mind to walk the waves' high road
until they've worn the surf to sleep and it is called
to turn and fall away, muttering its vengeance.

We have had the same battles: with trees that bend
us down who only mean to climb, with pools that know
no bottom we will touch despite our dives,
with ourselves, with what we want and cannot be
until things start we can't control, until the moon
like an old friend reaches out and turns our sea around.

GEOGRAPHY LESSON

Practice mouthing syllables just after the announcer.
Learn to spell from the headlines.
Speak the text as you read until your tongue curls up.
Roll the names out and away from you like tank treads,
        clear and unambiguous and foreign:
Cechnya, Al-Khader, Khasavyurt, Pyongyang.

It must have been this way in County Cork
for the Irish girls mastering the American,
that wondrous sound that swallowed up their uncles.
The girls would do the words to each other
the way the nuns had taught them how
to do the decades of the joyful mysteries.
Fingering the beads, they'd recite the names
enough until they wouldn't stumble once:
Appomattox, Antietam, Chickamauga, Manassas.

The thing that's good about this easy way
toward a knowledge of the world and all its places
is the certain promise of a new list coming soon,
strange sounds that come off the lips like prayer.

ARMY SAWBONES

We remove a lot of limbs in all the seasons.
The taking down has its own reasons

as compelling as the putting up, more studied too,
more art than science will accept, than craft construe,

this swift cut through the bone, tying off the trunk,
splicing roots together, lowering the hunk

of dead limb to the ground. It used to be that Spring
was slow. Few things break then, the sap sings

in limber boys. Here's one now. When he fell,
his taking down was carried off so well

the nerves won't sense for months the leg is gone.
They pulse useless to a brain knows the knuckled bone

will calce with its own boot the footless stump.
Those antique butchers, snow and freezing rain, we lump

with modern pains like napalm, hand grenades. We cut true
no matter what the cause. We are the civilizers, screw

the old bone to the new, synthetic shape, meld
the joint, send the soldered soldier home to mend.

Now the taking down owns all the seasons.
We saw limbs. All men own the reasons.

AIOI BRIDGE, HIROSHIMA, 1984

I remember still the old stone mason's mouth,
the way it carved a language out of sounds
my ears can see, the words are that bright,
the way those ancient incantations worked
like hands on building blocks he had found
to give away from what we all have lost.

He might well be Tiresias,
disguised this time around
as on old Japanese stone mason
to offer me a piece of what had been
Hiroshima, a hunk of wall that could
have come from Thebes. It is so cold.

As big as a loaf of unleavened bread,
another age's building block, this stone
and blessed in being here at all,
half of it blackened with the August rain
that rose from the ground like the dead.

The mason, his voice as high and hard
to read as birds, sang me a place
between the rivers to carry out
what could be found of the fatal city
fallen down and rising now around us.

I take away what was not made to stand
alone. I take it though I should think
to test the truth of the black rain
by biting down, or else I do bite down,
as metalmongers have taught me, and find out.

I take it though I think I've read that come
the night my tongue and gums will bleed
unstoppered through my broken, blackened teeth,
my chromosomes will wrinkle up with loss,
my eyes burn in a vast, unequal sun.

Afterwards, I scrub my hands for days
or else I don't. I forget even if I go
shamefaced to our customs clerk,
confess I have no rights to what I have,
confess I have another's loss as worthless gain.

ANTIETAM'S BLOODY LANE

The old woman from County Cork keens
For her sons who fell and broke
In a foreign place called Bloody Lane,
Boy-os who died in blood mud in Maryland
And will not be waked in their mother's parlor
Nor have the priest say the *Sanctus Sanctus
Sanctus* for their wedding Masses.

Some of the women will allow themselves anyway
To believe the Irish boys still live, have gone west
To gold and glory. Soon enough, over steeped tea
They promise the lads will send for them.
Soon enough, they will all be together
In Chicago, in Philadelphia, those odd
Sounding pieces of heaven.

Bloody Lane, men of too much mercy named it.
Bloody it is, and a wretched fine place for a brawl.
Picked at and primped as you never were
In life for your Wake, you get your ride
To a grave in the forgetting ground, the dry
Cold ground the Never Ending Ladies will keep
To work off days of Purgatory.

Better to fight with the other lads for a cause
You'd an inkling of and nothing more.
Better to go, as the Union Sergeant said,
Where you'll all be safe from Chicago's bitter cold
And a bed as empty as the English heart.

Bloody it is, the lane in Antietam,
And dark enough you could find
Your soul if you're looking to.

The sons of the sons of your uncles' sons
Will play the pipes of an evening for Bloody Lane
And for Gettysburg and for the end of you, you lads
Of County Cork and Kerry and old Mayo.

ADVICE TO WAR POETS

When working on a war poem,
Don't write in a pink book.
If you must do so, use
A livid red grease-stick
Or a shade of black
Sufficient to overwhelm
Any hint of sentiment.

Use no blush either to simulate
A dream of woman writing
A poem at night in a pink book
Whilst staring into a dark pool
For words that will jump out
Of the water into her mouth,
Lured by the lipstick,

down her gargled throat
and, in due course, through
her fingers to the pen, poised
as a weapon over paper.
In no case, let the words
be pink, which will not hide
the blood, blackening as it ages.

SAYING GOODBYE

We listen with our ties on straight,
hoping for once the end will change
or we will change, remember what
it means to want to listen when
we'd rather play at something else.
He builds the stories one by one
against the rest of a life that hasn't been,
for all he knows and cares, that great,

a past that now won't change no matter how
we want it to. Mostly what he tells us
are stories of the war, the Big One, WWII,
a sudden lifetime gone from him, a place
in France that smelled of garlic and a girl
he goes shy about each time. The oldest stories,
a stranger in town, a delicate, smiling girl,
and men who'd rather play than fight,
everything he knows to grace the time.

Before we put our suit coats on,
he tells us brothers stories he has
this minute remembered, details
he adds to amuse or teach or both.
His face floods with memory
so full his voice drops off
to yesterday, gets itself together,
comes home to us to stay.

NAVAL BOMBARDMENT

What changes is what lives. The uncharged shell
snug in its barrel is not yet conceived. The fact
is there as sure as tomorrow whaling in the belly
of a virgin, but to send the shell changing
through air, across the watching water,
requires several thousand years of lust,
compacted into one skilled seaman's thrust,
one burped ejaculation. The 16 inch gun fires
and deep in the belly of the land the egg
drops to meet the falling shell. You can't,
they say in wardrooms after breakfast,
you can't make an omelette without breaking eggs.
What lives is being changed. Charge the shell.

CRANES IN FLIGHT OVER WARSAW

She looked up, expecting enemy shells with nails
As decoration, close enough that she could count
The points, close enough she could imagine the hurt,
Remembering the ways her parents died,
How they welcomed what they could not want,
How slow the dying was, how filled with grace.

She looked again and saw the birds, as gentle in flight
As wisps of air, as needed as air in a breathless room.
They were flying south, a Vee of harmony,
Sky-scullers, sewing the world together as they went,
Going home, going away, pulling the moment with them.

She looked up, expecting birds, and saw the shells
Disappear, and then again the birds, cranes they were,
Carrying tomorrow in their beaks. One scratched
An itch in flight, the strangest thing she saw all year,
then took the wind in her face for the other cranes.

AFTER THE BATTLE AT SEVEN PINES

Sometimes, after the guns had stilled,
We would hear a girl laugh, the sound
as strange as frogs in the flour bin.
Those two days at Seven Pines,
it seemed as if we forgot how to smile.

Smiling, I figured, was a foreign thing
That needed muscles I didn't have,
All of mine having gone to hiding out,
Ducking down, sliding through mud
That grabbed me with a hundred hands.

I'd like to meet the man from North or South
Could laugh and mean it after Seven Pines.
Fair Oaks, some folks call it, but that was later.
He'd have a different place to stand than mine,
Or be a little mad, which I could understand.

JONATHAN EDWARDS IN THE WOODSHED

Trees have freedom, Goody, though they turn
Toward the sun against the laws of furniture,
Amaze the ministering eye with their need to be.
You know the tree in our parish yard that bends
At right angles back against itself,
Then shoots off as if it is an hypotenuse
Away from the rights of normal trees to head
straight down and up to what they need.

Things do get in the way, they do:
an overhanging branch, an ache that starts
with the bad seed, a wanton want that alters sense
to satisfy. A path I walked today for guidance
had trees that corkscrewed up. A hickory
wrapped around another tree and climbed,
finding the littlest only way and holding fast
its course against the needs of gravity.

A little like us, the trees, but not a lot.
Our freedom is governed by direction,
Goodman. If hell is where we are bent,
a temperate heaven being found
may be despised for what it isn't.

THE MAN WITH THE HOE AT THE GETTY MUSEUM

Jean-Francois Millet 1862

Except for the sackcloth blouses
His wife has stitched together
From the gut of last year's cow,

Except for a club he leans on
To keep him almost vertical
Who otherwise would fall
Down into a spiral of hardscrabble
Except for the thick peasant shoes
That fan out like cudgels, like art,

Except for the wisps of smoke
Behind him, rising to blend
With the gray blue sky of LA,
Except for his eyes that now and then
Saw something as well and clearly
As man could and could name it
Before it went away,

Except for Millet, except for Millet
The tourist who passes, scratching his arms
In wonder in the way of immigrants
To a rich country, scratching his behind
To stir deadened blood and fat
To join the working brain,

Except for Millet, the man from the customized bus
Would never, nor could he, name
What he saw, what he for a moment became.

MARY CASSATT

You know how some parties aren't parties
at all, how she will have to sit in a boat
for hours, overdressed, a baby in her lap,
a small smile you have learned can taste
like poison on her lips.

You are aware of the shoreline he approaches
blind, his back turned at the oars' command.
You see the steep city that teeters on rock
and, to the left, the road that empties on the sky.

You would like some to believe that it is Sunday,
that the sky and the water are as blue as paint,
that she, with her only family, is on a boating party.

Over his shoulder, though, you let her see what is coming.
You slash her red mouth shut, let her say nothing at all.

COBLENTZ'S FARM

after a painting by Walt Bartman

It's as good a way as any to plant
A farm against the rolling hills
Of Frederick County. Just get
A herd of milking cows to hold
The meadow down and a Boss cow, bold
Enough to stand alone, to show them how
To find their way to the milking shed
And the farmer's mothering hands.

Bluewash the fence that's only there
To keep the cows content and let
The long arm of the road bend in comfort
around the hickory trees and toward the house
That hides itself behind the barns.

While you're at the painting chore, you might
As well bluewash the roofs of the buildings too,
As soft reminders of the sky that's home
To traveling clouds. The cows will tell you how
To measure the hours before each night.
The deepening blue will tell you of the years.

If I were you I'd get myself an artist man,
Pay him a bucket of milk warm from the teats
To put the softness of the farm in solid terms.
He will know to let the cowgate burn a little red,
To have the shade fall like tongues toward the cows
And lick the meadow to a coolness after noon sun.

So the neighbors can see how things are on your farm,
I'd have him paint that Boss cow red and white
To shine like a beacon, and shape a fence

That's meant to keep nobody in or out
Unless it happens you're a cow. I'd tell him last
To let the road broaden its welcome as it ends,
To let the canvas dress the walls of memory
And lead us back who have been long away.

THE BURGHERS OF CALAIS

Rodin's burghers in the sun
are no less men than when
they stood in mud or snow.
Their faces are more fluid, sure.
Bronze glints off the foreheads.

One neck, exposed and bent,
glistens in the afternoon,
but changed? No, not at all,
not utterly, not the way
they changed in Calais.

Two look straight on, but down,
not willing anymore to meet
the little pity of passers-by.
One turns as if to speak against
his shoulder, maybe to the man

behind, who turns himself away.
His arms are dropped weights
that will not ever rise again.
His empty palms face out
the way a child's will

when he has nothing left
against the father's rage.
To his left, a fifth man throws
his right arm up as if to block
a blow, his left side staggers.

He sags above a key he holds,
too heavy for an earthly thing.
The last man bows his head into

both hands and, standing, starts
a fall that will not stop.

II

In Spring, the Burghers
lose their way no less
than fall, are almost warm
enough to loosen up.

They won't though, not now,
not when Rodin has stopped
them cold and left them there,
almost leaning on each other.

In winter, they don't put on
their overcoats, don't shiver
at the sky. Summer's always been
their season, when they shine.

III

They're set almost by chance. In Washington
we often take directions by their stance,
caught like them between Capitol and monument.
Two, almost beside each other, straighten
toward the north. To their east, there's one
who turns as if to make one final plea toward

what follows him. The southern figure looks
north and west. The one who's mostly lost
looks out in what is not a mock despair.
There's one of them who holds his head
in both hands and his eyes on the ground
which is only fixed as long as you look.

IV

They stand there still. Look closer,
there's not a one of them but moves.
Like time, they stand there, like stone.

In the middle, a puddle forms, a
water glazed as they. Though we've
had sun all day, it lasts till dusk,

caught in that little place
at the dead center of the six
who remain the burghers of Calais

though a hundred years have passed
since they've been thrown together
and bid, Be still, Be still.

THE EGG MAN IN WARSAW

After Z. Beksinski's No. 26

Having painted what he could only see
Through fingers sharpened on the wheel of war
Turned in a city he would leave as men must,
He went home to eat for man must eat
And lay with his wife in a feather bed

> For man must pretend to sleep in the end.
> Body to body they lay and prayed that death
> When it came would take away their bones
> With their skin, with their will always to eat
> And procreate, always to make dreams

Out of the emptied city. Bombed emptied squares
Stared where his parents used to meet their friends
For some quiet talk. What he found to draw
Was the perfect shape that is an egg, A head
In blacks and whites and blood of a man

> Of bones making his way across the city.
> Now this is the nightmare, he thought,
> For he knows that an egg is not a predator
> Though arms and legs grow from it,
> He knows that the egg is his Polish neighbor

And that the blood egg of his neighbor's face,
Swathed in impermanent hospital gauze,
Couldn't be, couldn't ever be more than it is,
And when he awoke, as he had to, he went
Directly to Wenceslaw Square and there it was

> Walking like any old nightmare, bones crouched
> For good or ill, and not at all ashamed to be seen so,
> The egg being where he started from, rich fruit
> Of rich thighs given to peace, thighs offered in love.
> Overhead, birds flew, who did not want to be included.

FINDING LOSS IN A FLEMISH SCHOOL
Teniers the Younger, "Boors Carousing"

Two of them sit as they've been told,
one stands dead center, pretending.
The three have each their pipes, long tubes
of whitened clay they pull at, we can guess,
for their pleasure and their pain.
A fourth man takes this chance to piss,
his back and shoulders hunched
against the worst kinds of surprise.

Teniers the Younger puts right the way
men brace their necks against ill winds
since the world of standing men began.
A fifth man has disappeared, up canvas left.
a broken piece of crockery follows him
out the door. Emptiness abides in all
the pipe bowls, in the emptied dishes,
in the emptying lines of the painting
Teniers has fixed before us.

The spaces men can never quite fill up,
Or find excuse for emptying,
Delineate this painting by Teniers,
such studies as an artist practices
if he's to be past master at
        the quiet constancy of loss
that makes the little gains men make so rich.

ARTISAN

A man whose only left arm
has been stroked by his brain
into a stillness beyond his power
to command or change and hangs still,
waiting for what will and will not come,
this man, this stroked man,
is helping his young son dig a hole
in the sand, using his feet as hands,
his legs as arms. The man's an artisan,
shaping what the boy knows
will swallow the ocean.

With clenched toes, the man
routes for them a quick escape
in case the water thinks to do
what water may. He knows the way
a little flooding here and there can hurt
a summer hole beyond redemption,

Though if they have to start again
from scratch, with buckets and tools,
his son will remember
what sand has never thought
and teach the artisan anew how to put
aside what has been done
and find his happiness in absences.

GUERNICA AT THE MUSEUM

We concede to the painting we have before us
that soon we will tire even of this lucidity
and need to walk in the sun of the Mall.
The rockets, we are told, face toward Silver Spring
And Fairfax. Inside the cone, we are safe.

Guernica is clean and free from random writing.
The frame does not intrude on what is art.
True, the figures weird the eye.
Is there something to be remembered here?
Whatever shall we do with what we see?

Our guide says to bring the eye in closer,
To notice the colors, how they bulk and smear.
Better, he says, to notice that
than what is being thought,
Better still to walk into the sun while you can.

The gun-ships circle our public places
like beneficent birds. They would never fire
where we are, we are assured by public faces,
Can go back to the gallery to study beauty
Wrought from common things: a small girl at a fence,
a field of flowers here, pieces of dead men there.

PRACTICING THE ART IN NEW JERSEY

"The profound change has come upon them"
                                    W.C. Williams

You, baby doctor,
pulling boys out
by their toes, finding two
or three baby girls up your sleeve
by legerdemain, getting
it all down to a science,
I hear you have plumbed
a couple of poems
the other morning, put
them down on the pad
you use to prescribe
the medicines we need.

That's an artful thing
to do, making changes
that matter, getting them
underway the way
you've been taught,
giving us all a chance
we would not have had
without that little tug
toward a change that you,
you baby doctor, prescribed
in your hot medicinal scrawl.

TEHRAN HOD-CARRIER

Doubled up for good and all, a mathematic
he has been taught by an excess of brick,
and a deficiency of calcium in the bones,

the Persian hod-man, with a mother
who has worn a sari all her days and nights,
even in bed, even at the moment of his conception,

and a wife who wears high heels and walks
a poodle to prove she is a modern woman
and proud of the life she has stitched together,

the hod man has—even bent to brick—
the common sense not to show a mean obeisance
to mullahs or puffy businessmen.

Turned earthward as he is, he has trained himself
to focus as few of us have chance or pleasure
on the industry and the friendly ways of ants.

He is long past straightening out. He does
What he does, taught by ants and saints,
despite the emptying stares of the money men

who require to be obeyed, with only the ladder rungs
curled to hold him, and as he climbs he will sing
for reasons I can not—though I have tried—construe.

FATBACK

Her father loved fatback, a thick slab
Of pig fat cut from the wallow that remained
After the pig had gone, as we had prayed, to heaven.
The fatback sat for weeks in the brown ice-box
When he went traveling to sell Dynamic Shoes
So the kids could survive the depressing time
They were due to spend before they grew away.

She would stand and ache for forbidden tastes
At the open door and stare at the dripping wall
Behind the lettuce and swelling milk
With a thirst beyond redemption. She had been told
What that fatback would do to her mouth and throat,
That it was meant for fathers only.
Her oldest brother would tell the oldest story
Of where fatback came from and set the young ones
To trembling sleep. The son who ran away
Took chunks of ice and chewed them for energy
But left the fatback pouting on the shelf.

And when the father returned, having sold
Enough and no more, the kitchen rang
With happy sounds and the sweet smell of grease
swallowed the corner where the mouse slept
Dreaming of being a rat. She laughed
At the father's faces building the heat,
She laughed at herself for her grief,
Told stories of school and the trees
That pleased him enough and no more.
The mother shooed her to bed at last
But she watched from the steps as the father ate
And was proud as a mother mouse for the food
Meant for her eating, saved for him alone.

THE SCIENTIST'S PRAYER

After Maurice Maeterlinck, *The Hive and the Bee*

The circle of the horizon beckons
And I am helpless to attend its call
And, blinded by the stars' light,
I waken to the galaxies within
This earth of all earths, stunned
to sight by god's design.

The circles beckon and demand.
If the blind man knows, he does not speak,
And the horizon has been calm for years
Beyond the telling. What I must do
is what the gull does: rest on the jut

Of jetty, wait for the moment of love
Then rise and dive beyond the self—
Land, sea and air are his elements
And mine. Much depends on faith,
I know and the circle of beckoning

Is round. The stars lean above, beyond
My reach. The belly of a bee's hive
Must be my little hope toward heaven.

SPIDER WEBS

The girl who loved spider webs
Had much to mull with herself.

She wondered at the two strands
Of anchoring the spider makes

And why she smelled rock when she saw
A web grow between the sliced hills.

Before she knew about the boys,
Their stone-sure hearts,

Their spinning hands, she tried
Her skill at weaving a spider-web

But couldn't get the knack so turned
At last to soccer in the far field.

Rocky-thin and safe from mountains
And smart enough to shelter from thunder,

She would kick the ball to herself
At the other end, then run like a boy

Had never done and kick it back again.
In the early morning, the webs would work

At gathering the mist and pretending
That their design was beauty, nothing more.

Some flies got fooled, but she never did,
Not once in all the years she kicked that ball

And ran after it. After those apprenticeships,
She studied mountains for their art and brought

A man to herself who knew to kick a ball as hard
as she did and could gentle a spider in his hand.

GOAT FARMING AT FLAT ROCK

Carl Sandburg liked a little honey
in his morning coffee which he never drank
till afternoon, a proper time for a poet to rise
who had been at it half the night.
He took some goat's milk to lighten the cup,
give the coffee a taste worth looking toward.

His wife rose early, raised prize goats from the go,
the get, fed the kids two at a time in the cold kitchen
she'd had built at Connemara, a name they kept
because it fit. In a single year, one of those prize goats
produced forty seven hundred pounds of milk,
a Flat Rock record that may stand as long as goats give milk.

Carl weighed the words he meant to use each week.
They lifted off the scales like bees, would not stay put for anything,
as busy as his language had the need to be
trying to prise itself from traps. He woke late, snuck up on syllables
that swelled like honeyed hives, milked them through the nights
among the rocks, stroked them, honeybee and goat, into the poem.

BEYOND THE HOT SUN

The old man who lives alone near the sea
can only make things out in certain light,
with eyes that love old men and horizons.
The rest of us will have to learn the grace
of growing, how it is to look beyond the hot
sun, how to let the eye feel the way
toward what it will with luck become.

The old man wraps the scarf of night around him
and lifts it off for morning work. He is content
to do his stretching exercises, limbering up
for the long walk he means to take
before he shakes himself like an old dog,
gives the ocean a drink of his plenitude,
lets himself be seen by us for what he is,
and shrugs for what he isn't anymore.

WEATHERING THE FRONT DOOR

Ah. For the deep heaven's sake,
I'm fed up entirely.
Let's have an Irish door, at least,
if we can't have the brawn and the stout
and the smell of peat in the house.

You pick the paint, I'll slap it on,
a cardinal red lacquered sheen
with brass to announce and brass
to let in and the hinges too, brass,
swinging as bold as the money
down the street.

   Remember how we practiced for the wedding
   after the last sun storm of earliest spring
   had sworn off and headed up to Boston.
   Took the door down, we did, the way it went up,
   flipped it flat on the spring onions starting to sprout,
   waxed it so our feet would shine and snap.

To qualify our steps for heaven,
when late spring springs its tricks,
we'll take down the door again and put
our dancing shoes on, the taps of them
beating a jig and a reel into the air, give us
a walking out together above the dirt
like we are more than man and woman.

It's a way of letting the neighbors know
of the merry mischief to come, this taking down
the door. It's a way of letting the feet fly

that would be stuck and held in the mud.
We'll only be taking it down at last to celebrate
the goings-on of those worth going on about:

but when we do we'll drop it right outside
the threshhold so the bride and groom can reel
from the garden path into the house and bed,
can hear the young ones tapping up their heels
and toes and us ourselves singing so boisterous loud
the words echo off the ground and the answering sky.
Having occasions it is. Why we have the front doors.

GRAVITIES

Got nose to nose with ants, I did,
to get our signals straight about our needs.
Came eye to bulged eye with a hungry frog
Thrust beyond himself for living's sake.

When I saw the ways things work,
I tried the boneyard stumble,
letting my whole sack of immortality
and noble thoughts—my serene self itself

come separately to a ground as hard
as pulled triggers on elbow and knee.
Try falling once yourself, astonished man,
as natural as tomorrow, and stagger up

all aches and crinks and joy at having them.
Now, then, to the wobble of wheel, the hill
that means to keep us in our place,
the parachute, the wizardry of rain.

APPRENTICE CHEF

Growing a fruit salad for dessert,
the stolid apples, being first and hard,
the heart of them gone, as base,
he daydreamed about the seamstress
who pinned his left ankle to the cuff
and smiled up at him with orange lips.

The plump grapes as complacent
as churchgoers, the kiwi bragging
their wide smiles of fertility,
all that sweetness, so many seeds,
he sliced the tip of his index finger off
and couldn't find it anywhere,
guessed what was beginning.

STILL LIFE PHOTOGRAVURE

There are no people in the room,
No people at the window looking out,
Just you and I looking in.

The people who make the judgments
About people in the little town
Prefer not to show their faces,

Would like to remain out of it,
Would rather not hear the problems,
Are late for an important occasion.

The little people in the town
Are not here either. They would not
Be comfortable, nor would you or I

Who only love peace and the time and space
We have to look in on the slight hill
And the town as real as we would have it,

Nestled at its foot the light of memory
Sliding toward The Old Hat Bar & Grille,
The Five and Dime as shined as shoes.

HILDA AND ME AND HAZEL

These stories are as true as clocks
though there are some in this town
think I would make up the goings-on
just so I would have my say.
What we are about is partly underground
and partly overhead, or that what was.

Happens I catch myself a baby mockingbird,
get him right here in this hand closed up,
his whole body shaking like some old
jalopy Ford that needs a tune-up bad,
his tail feathers tickling my palm
like he is a girl wants something that
I got and she don't. I hear that once
it smells of people, the mother won't
have nothing more to do with it,
so I start to pull the feathers off,
one at a time, stacking them up
real careful in a matchbox that I keep
against emergencies like this, figuring if
I catch enough of them this year maybe
I will stuff myself a pillow for my head
and maybe one for Hilda and for Hazel too.
Like any damned fool, which some will say
my mother didn't raise none of, I take
my eyes away from what I am doing for a sec
when wham! that mother mocker's at my eye
pulling like we are playing at a tug of war.
The mother makes toward the middle branch.
I'm off my feet by now, then something snaps
like a whole string of rubberbands has broke
and I am back on the ground where I began.

I only need the one eye anyway, though things
have flattened some, the way I see it now.

The next one, Hilda likes. She says it shows
that fools is fools in uniform or not.
So the story is a fat black snake that curls
around our cellar water tank like it
is desperate ripe in love or similar to that.
The snake will not let go despite
the talking to I give it good, from me
who undisputable do not take to snakes.
So I have to get the police here
to get it gone and the police says
he would have to have my social security
first, the number, before he could go below
the ground floor, says it is a rule.
Finally I give the number up. He goes,
beating his stick on each of the going down
steps, hollering like Calvin by god Coolidge
is the President. The snake by then is gone as gold
but that doesn't stop the police from taking out
his .45 and shooting about two and one-half
holes straight through the hot water heater
plus the one bullet that bounces all around
like Willy Masconi's triple cushion trick
until that bullet finds the furnace wall that spits
out soot and flame enough to set the house to fire.
The local Hose and Ladder Company alarm
themselves to help things out. It's me
could tell them how to put a fire down,
could tell them how to use a shovel too.
Anyhow, the next unwelcome guest that calls,

we make our mind up there and then will best
be dealt with by ourselves, my sisters who
you will hear about and me, who is Henry
that you already know don't take too much
of prompters to tell his side of things.

So this story is the skunk.
My sister Hazel grabs the softball bat.
Hilda, who is the other sister, ankle yanks
her wading boots. We head outside,
me with the bullet gun in the lead and she
and she behind to sight the polecat out for us
because of my flat eye and everything about
the gun. We've had about enough of the skunk
who has put his smell beneath our sitting porch
as if he means to stay and be one of us,
or start a family of his own to add
to the general stink of things. I circle back
toward the front, my gun cradled to my gut,
tipping toe like I was showed. Hazel's 53,
still sets her hair in curlers every day,
turning the hangs around like they was snakes.
Hilda, who is the other, doesn't damned well care
about much of anything except her feet and keeping
them away from that that bites or cuts or stings,
or, as in the present case, that stinks.
My tobacco's caught where it can give
me juice the times I need a shot of it,
especially just before I shoulder up my .22,
take aim. Sister Hazel's curler spikes,
they're green, same as the halter she
puts on—to brighten up the place, she says.

Hilda, the other one, plays the piano accordian
in her boots, two tunes she has learned
by heart and by pecking at the keys
so they're and we're about worn out
from the acculturation.

Skunks is skunks, I say, no matter what.
Happens that Hazel, her with the soft heart
and the bat as mean as her head, starts around
the other side, beating on the ground enough
to wake the dead that are not, quite.
I am talking here about our neighbors to the west,
city folks, the ones I mean to get to next.
Now, here comes this skunk looking almost
too small for his smell, hopping like the fool
and baby rabbit our own mother showed up with
one Easter week and promptly died, as if we cared.
So now the skunk is running toward Hilda's foot,
her with the Sears and Roebuck guaranteed-rubber
knee-high wading boots. I shoot as if I mean to,
leading the skunk the way my uncle Billy taught me.
Same as most other times, I miss.
The bullet skitters like a flat rock
skimming water. Hazel shrieks out loud
like it is somebody she knows been shot.
The gun remembers what it sounds like,
lets the neighbors know that everything is O.K.
and that their skunk, the one they meant to give
away, is coming back across the road from us to them.

After dinner (Hazel sets the extra place
just, she says, in case), we will sit and sort
things out, remember how we always know

to work together, all of us, willynilly,
working like we did, had to, the time
that Hazel had herself a man come calling
that I did not know and did not like
no matter what and I surprised my own self
and them with what I did and did not miss.
The ground we stuck it in beneath the porch
is soft, the smell's near gone for good and all.
No snakes, no skunks, no nothing underground
or overhead that stops us three from getting on.

The thing about the baby mockingbird,
the thing that really gets me is,
the wind came up and all the feathers flew.
Sweet Jesus, I'd have liked to seen them go,
flying on their own, making like they were whole.

DOORMAN

The night we heard the news from space,
my daughter, who is three, remarks
with no surprise but careful to instruct:
"The moon is like a doorknob,"
to that other self all children seem
to have and have to answer to.

I sit trying to construct a poem of praise.
Spacemen and women stumble down the page.
She says again, impatient to be gone,
"The moon's a doorknob," and,
already dressed to play outside,
waits for me to open up the sky.

ENOUGH

Some callers are so slow we've got
to speed them up. One of us will say
You couldn't go any slower, could you?
They're smart, they'll get it. They don't,
they're gone. Enough's, we say, enough.

We lay our cards out in a square
three deep, hitch our chairs toward
the long wobble of a table. We're here to play
Bingo. B-I-N-G-O. God's game.
We'll win some money too. Some of us.

There's one of us, just one, but one
is all we need, will say God Bless You
loud enough when anybody'd sneeze to where
we none of us could hear the number called
and then we have to yell repeat, repeat.

We used to use sunflower seeds to mark
the numbers we had luck enough to have.
Now plastic's mostly what they've got,
not worth a darn for chewing on but good
enough for keeping track of where we are.

Sometimes she'll say God Bless so much
one of us will tell her, that's enough.
She'll simmer down then but we can hear
her lips working overtime, blessing us
who came to lose what we can't keep.

One time she won three straight Bingos
in a row. You'd think her husband—

which she hasn't got—had hit the lottery
for real. One more, that's all I ask,
she said. Well, we hoped for her enough

she should have won all night, that time.
We leaned toward her, each and all of us,
wishing her a card she'd never drawn,
wishing her seeds enough to fill the letter X,
the letter Y, the letter Z, just everything.

THE SEASON AFTER AND JUST BEFORE

Those days I need my fortune told,
I turn to Autumn, oracle,
old season wise and young enough
to carry still the warmth of used to be.

She takes off her hat, her sweater, everything
that might get in the way of sensing what's ahead,
of sensing out the world's luck, just exactly what
we have got ourselves into since the spring

when everything that mattered glowed
straight through the mud and blossomed.
I rub my hand sometimes, a ritual,
around my other hand, a little trick

the doctors say is a sign I lack some vitals
others in my family have in abundance
and maybe they will lend me some.
I doubt it, knowing my family's tendencies

and ask old autumn could I rub her old head
instead, feel the smart bumps she has that say
there's weather up ahead for everybody
we won't be liking and won't be missing either

when it's gone and spring has come again
around the corner where the grocery store used to be,
smiling like flowers were the only thing worth eating
and sun, coat enough for anyone who fancies clothes.

First time I heard autumn talk so well, I knew
for all my hand-wringing, I were blessed
and my brothers, the ones who ate all the bacon,
might know the Latin but couldn't hear what I did.

Only autumn though. My time to shine.
Spring with all her babble about brooks and breaking codes
our elders had hidden in the closet, I couldn't read at all.
Sweating summer, when pretty girls sat out to boil

in their little fat, remains a mystery of mute to me,
and winter, cold commercial winter, too busy
to speak anything but snow and ice,
but autumn now and always, my time to shine.

There's others like me that the world
would like to dismiss. We bide our time
listening to voices others cannot hear.
We savor October becoming November.

CANDIDATE

Here's a man we could elect,
his wonderfully straightforward teeth
dropping toward the carrot,
no doubt at all about his appetite.
His resumé, his being itself
is pure American:
the friendly impertinence
of "What's up, Doc?"
the democratic urge
to know what's going on.

He dons his dove grey morning suit
as well as any diplomat,
reveals a nakedness that says
there's nothing here to hide or fear.
The world's a carrot to old Bugs.
An appetite for our time.
A ready hand for practical jokes,
some slapstick, the legerdemain
to pluck a carrot out of the air,
a stammer that hides the wise man.

The ever ready fall guy
is by his side ready to fool,
old Elmer Fudd, but love too,
love for being such a perfect flub
and bald and fat and short. A pal
we all should have. So when old Bugs
says "That's all, folks," with his wink,
we know he means that's all for now,
that we'll see him in the White House
if we only keep our wits about us.

THE SILENCE OF EGGS

He never told anyone at the monastery
How he talked to the chickens as he took
The warm eggs from under them,
How he forgave their beaks, their sharp
Reminders of the privileges of motherhood.
He never even told the tree he came to
For its murmuring shade to wipe his brow
Of the Iowa summer. His best friend
Kept the bees, was becoming one himself,
Talked to the queen, he once confessed,
In bee, the sweet melodics of a love
That made nothing of the hive but sense.

Once when he was forty-five his sister came
From the East to visit him. She was allowed
To sit with him at meals but not to talk to anyone,
To listen while they ate, listen and meditate
On the scripture the senior reader chose.
She told her children how the Trappists' teeth
Scraped as they tried to chew the broth,
How the rosary beads sounded like rattlesnakes,
How she was afraid the whole time she was there
Of what she had become, how far she'd gone
Away from this holy silence, so far that she heard
The rattle of the bones each time her brother walked.

We got a crate of freshfed, handpacked eggs
From the monastery every couple months
During the war. The cardboard cups we kids used
To save our favorite stones could take an egg from here
To Timbuktu and back again my older brother bragged
Who otherwise had nothing much to do with miracles.

Every week my mother cracked a half a dozen open
To scramble us our Sunday eggs, she'd listen hard
For the silence that came tumbling out. Best part
Of the week, she'd say. That silence. Safe
In her own kitchen, among her gang of galoots
Who found in noise the harmonies of being young,
She would hide the silence of the eggs away
So she could have it with her afternoon tea.
She sometimes said when we were gone
She'd take the cloth, tuck herself inside a shell,
Not say another word till evening broke.

THE PURPOSES OF CIRCUSES

I used to know a guy, at least I wish I did
Who could stand on one finger for a minute flat.

I never said he could dance at the same time,
Did I? I never said I really knew him,

But I saw him once at the Greatest Show
On Earth. Saw him true

With these very eyes. I even got to counting down
Or counting up depending on your numbers system

Fifty one, fifty two, like that. And by the end,
I was cheering like raspberries were in season.

I tried it once myself when I was in the Navy
And full of beans. Had a swabbie pal hold my legs

Up toward the stars and said now watch this watch
And broke my middle finger then my nose flat out.

One thing they never teach you about circus tricks:
Actually, a couple things… but then you grow up

And you either know or you don't you were meant
To marry the girl on the flying trapeze or you weren't

And that kids should show off when they're young,
And when they get older, they shouldn't.

NOTE ON THE AUTHOR

Martin Galvin's *Wild Card*, Washington Writers'
Publishing House (WWPH), won the 1989 Columbia
Prize, judged by then U.S. Poet Laureate Howard
Nemerov. His poems have been included in numerous
national journals and anthologies including *Best
American Poetry 1997, Poetry,* and *The Atlantic
Monthly.* In addition to *Sounding the Atlantic* and his
book *Wild Card,* he has published three chapbooks.
Awards for his work include First Prize for "Hilda and
Me and Hazel" in *Poet Lore's* narrative poetry contest
in 1992, First Prize in *Potomac Review's* Best Poem
Competition in 1999 for "Freight Yard at Night," and First
Prize from *Sow's Ear Poetry Journal* for "Cream" in a
2007 national competition. Galvin holds a doctorate in
American Literature from the University of Maryland. He
recently served as Book Review Editor for *Poet Lore* for
five years. For August of 2007, he was awarded a writer's
residency at Yaddo. He lives, with his wife Theresa, in
Chevy Chase, Maryland, and Ocean View, Delaware. He
can be reached at Galvinhimself@yahoo.com

Breinigsville, PA USA
26 April 2010
236853BV00001B/6/P